READERS

Rainforests

Focus: Habitats

Meredith Costain

Rainforests are hot, rainy places with lots of trees. Some trees grow so high that it's very dark near the ground.

Thousands of plants and animals make the rainforest their home.

Some rainforest trees grow to the very top of the rainforest. Big roots under the ground help them grow so tall.

Many tall trees
grow very close together.
The rainforest floor is
very shady and dark.

But most rainforest plants
still need sunlight to live.
So, some rainforest plants
grow very big leaves
to gather more sun.

Some rainforest plants
climb out of the dark.
They climb up the trees
to get the sunlight they need.

Many rainforest plants have
bright, beautiful colors.
Their bright colors
make them easy to see.

Some rainforest animals need to find the colorful plants. The animals eat the colorful plants to help them grow.

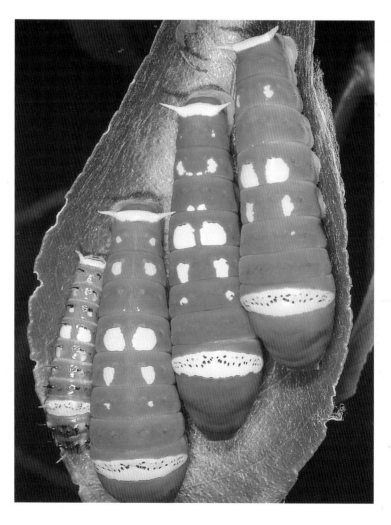

Some rainforest animals are predators. Predators hunt other animals for food.

But many rainforest animals
have learned to
live in the trees.
Some animals climb
or swing from
treetop to treetop.

Rainforest birds have bright colors and are noisy. They use their color and noise to find each other in the trees.

Rainforest snakes are the same color as the trees. They use their color to hide in the trees.

The rainforest floor is dark.
Some rainforest animals
use their colors and
patterns to find each other.

When people cut down the rainforest, many animals lose their homes. People are learning to leave the rainforest alone.

Index